SandCastle™

First Rhymes

The Sub Club

Pam Scheunemann

Consulting Editor, Diane Craig, M.A./Reading Specialist

Published by ABDO Publishing Company, 4940 Viking Drive, Edina, Minnesota 55435.

Printed in the United States.

Credits
Edited by: Pam Price
Curriculum Coordinator: Nancy Tuminelly
Cover and Interior Design and Production: Mighty Media
Photo Credits: AbleStock, Corel, Photodisc

Library of Congress Cataloging-in-Publication Data

Scheunemann, Pam, 1955-
     The sub club / Pam Scheunemann.
         p. cm. -- (First rhymes)
     Includes index.
     ISBN 1-59679-533-6 (hardcover)
     ISBN 1-59679-534-4 (paperback)
         1. English language--Rhyme--Juvenile literature. I. Title. II. Series.

PE1517.S459 2005
808.1--dc22

2005048808

SandCastle™ books are created by a professional team of educators, reading specialists, and content developers around five essential components that include phonemic awareness, phonics, vocabulary, text comprehension, and fluency. All books are written, reviewed, and leveled for guided reading and early intervention reading, and designed for use in shared, guided, and independent reading and writing activities to support a balanced approach to literacy instruction.

Let Us Know

After reading the book, SandCastle would like you to tell us your stories about reading. What is your favorite page? Was there something hard that you needed help with? Share the ups and downs of learning to read. We want to hear from you! To get posted on the ABDO Publishing Company Web site, send us e-mail at:

sandcastle@abdopub.com

SandCastle Level: Beginning

-ub

chub

club

cub

sub

tub

This is a .

Here is our .

This is a  .

Here is a .

This is a  .

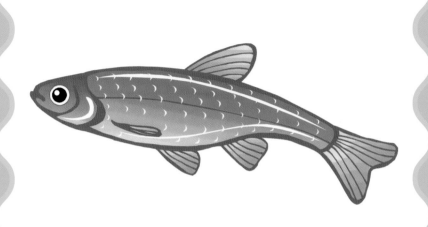

This fish is a chub.

Our club is fun.

A cub is soft.

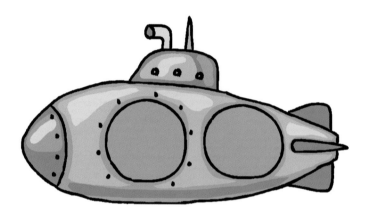

A sub floats
in the water.

You take a
bath in a tub.

The Sub Club

There is a little cub.

The little cub
has a gray toy sub.

The little cub
takes his sub
to a fun club.

The little cub
with the sub
meets a chub
at the sub club.

The little cub
and the chub
play in the tub
with all of the
sub club!

About SandCastle™

A professional team of educators, reading specialists, and content developers created the SandCastle™ series to support young readers as they develop reading skills and strategies and increase their general knowledge. The SandCastle™ series has four levels that correspond to early literacy development in young children. The levels are provided to help teachers and parents select the appropriate books for young readers.

Emerging Readers
(no flags)

Beginning Readers
(1 flag)

Transitional Readers
(2 flags)

Fluent Readers
(3 flags)

These levels are meant only as a guide. All levels are subject to change.

To see a complete list of SandCastle™ books and other nonfiction titles from ABDO Publishing Company, visit www.abdopub.com or contact us at:
4940 Viking Drive, Edina, Minnesota 55435 • 1-800-800-1312 • fax: 1-952-831-1632